# HIDDEN IN PLAIN SIGHT

A Journey of Autism, Motherhood, and Self-Discovery + *A step-by-step guide on how to love a neurodivergent adult*

## BY AMINA PHELPS

All rights reserved under the international and Pan-American copyright conventions.

First published in the United States of America.

All rights reserved. With the exception of brief quotations in a review, no part of this book may be reproduced or transmitted, in any form, or by any means, electronic or mechanical (including photocopying), nor may it be stored in any information storage and retrieval system without written permission from the publisher.

## DISCLAIMER

The advice contained in this material might not be suitable for everyone. The author designed the information to present her opinion about the subject matter. The reader must carefully investigate all aspects of any business decision before committing to him or herself. The author obtained the information contained herein from sources she believes to be reliable and from her own personal experience, but she neither implies nor intends any guarantee of accuracy. The author is not in the business of giving legal, accounting, or any other type of professional advice. Should the reader need such advice, he or she must seek services from a competent professional. The author particularly disclaims any liability, loss, or risk taken by individuals who directly or indirectly act on the information contained herein. The author believes the advice presented here is sound, but readers cannot hold her responsible for either the actions they take, or the risk taken by individuals who directly or indirectly act on the information contained herein.

Published by 1BrickPublishing
Printed in the United States
Copyright © 2024 by Amina Phelps
ISBN 978-1949303711

## DEDICATION

To AJ, whose journey inspired this book and whose unwavering spirit continues to teach me the true meaning of resilience and love. Your unique perspective on the world is a gift that I cherish every day.

To Taylor, my firstborn, whose presence in my life reminds me daily of the power of love, perseverance, and the endless possibilities that lie within us all. You are my constant source of pride and inspiration.

To all the Black women and girls on the autism spectrum, whose stories have been overlooked for far too long. This book is for you, to shine a light on your experiences and to honor your strength and courage.

To my husband, who has supported me through every challenge and triumph, and to the extended family and community members who have enriched my life with their love and wisdom.

And to every parent, educator, and ally who strives to understand and support neurodivergent individuals. May this book serve as a guide and a beacon of hope in your journey toward creating a more inclusive and compassionate world.

## DEDICATION REQUEST

Please share this book with anyone who you feel would benefit from its guidance, inspiration, and actionable steps for fostering understanding, empathy, and lasting connections with neurodivergent individuals.

# TABLE OF CONTENTS

Foreword: Embracing the Spectrum: A Tribute to Neurodivergent Brilliance and the Power of Love ............................. 1

Introduction: The Invisible Spectrum: Black Women and Girls in Autism Research ......... 7

## PART ONE: THE JOURNEY OF AUTISM AND SELF-DISCOVERY. ................. 13

Chapter 1: The Diagnosis that Changed Everything ................................ 15

Chapter 2: Revisiting The Past: Early Signs and Coping Mechanisms. ...................... 23

Chapter 3: Missed Signs and Misunderstood Behaviors ................................ 39

Chapter 4: Masking and Navigating Adulthood. ..................... 57

Chapter 5: Embracing Neurodiversity - The Moment of Self-Discovery and Acceptance .... 63

## PART TWO: A STEP-BY-STEP GUIDE ON HOW TO LOVE AND SUPPORT A NEURODIVERGENT ADULT ........... 73

Chapter 6: Understanding Neurodiversity:
Neurodiversity 101..........................75

Chapter 7: Building Meaningful Relationships
..........................................105

Chapter 8: Supporting Neurodivergent Adults in
Romantic Relationships ....................111

Chapter 9: Family, Friendship, and
Social Support.............................121

Chapter 10: Workplace Inclusion and Support for
Neurodivergent Individuals .................129

Chapter 11: Advocacy and Allyship ..........141

Chapter 12: Self-Care and
Continuous Learning........................151

Conclusion: Embracing Neurodiversity.......157

Appendix A: Neurodiversity Glossary .......163

Appendix B: Resources and
Support Organizations......................169

# FOREWORD

# EMBRACING THE SPECTRUM: A TRIBUTE TO NEURODIVERGENT BRILLIANCE AND THE POWER OF LOVE

For years, autism and neurodivergence have been misunderstood, often labeled as limitations rather than seen for the strengths they embody. Society has long attached a stigma to being on the spectrum, treating it as something to "fix" instead of recognizing the extraordinary abilities it can bring. But what if we shifted our perspective? What if we saw autism not as a challenge but as a unique way of thinking that holds untapped potential? Throughout history, many of the world's most innovative minds were neurodivergent—brilliant thinkers who pushed boundaries, often misunderstood because they didn't fit societal norms. Their genius wasn't a flaw but a gift.

The reality is that neurodivergent individuals possess incredible strengths, and these abilities should be celebrated, not marginalized. People like Albert Einstein and countless others changed the world with their unique approaches to problem-solving and creativity. Yet, even today, many individuals with autism are overlooked or dismissed. It's time to break away from outdated perceptions and embrace the truth—that neurodivergence brings with it a spectrum of abilities that, when understood, can enhance not only individual lives but also the relationships we build.

This is where Amina's story comes in. Her journey as a neurodivergent Black woman is a powerful example of what it means to embrace one's true self and turn perceived challenges into strengths. By sharing her experiences, Amina offers a voice for those who have long been overlooked, guiding others to better understand the brilliance that often goes unseen. Through her vulnerability, she opens the door for all of us to learn more about neurodiversity and its incredible potential in both life and love.

In every relationship, we are given the gift of discovering more about ourselves through the other person. For me, that person is my wife, Amina. Watching her navigate the complexities of life with strength and grace has been a deeply humbling experience, one that has taught me the true meaning of resilience. She has never shied away from embracing her story, even when it meant facing the toughest of challenges. This book represents the culmination of that journey—the willingness to be vulnerable, to be seen, and to share the truth that has always been "hidden in plain sight."

Our relationship has shown me that true love is built on the foundation of self-awareness and acceptance. Amina's journey of self-discovery, particularly in understanding and embracing her neurodivergence, has transformed not just her life but our relationship. She taught me that knowing yourself—your strengths, your struggles, and your unique needs—especially in relationships, is the key to creating a bond that can withstand anything. This book embodies that lesson.

Amina has taken her personal story, her experiences as a neurodivergent Black woman, and created something that is not only informative but also life-changing. She is showing the world that understanding and embracing neurodiversity is not just a personal journey—it's a community effort. This book will save lives and relationships. It will open the eyes of those who may have never considered the challenges and beauty of neurodivergent individuals and offer them the tools to foster love, compassion, and acceptance.

Her courage to share these intimate parts of her life, especially about navigating relationships while embracing her neurodivergence, is a gift. I have watched her fight through the frustrations, celebrate the victories, and embrace the unknown with grace. I have learned so much from her about how crucial it is to understand that not everyone sees the world the same way—and that's a beautiful thing. Whether you're neurodivergent or not, this book offers valuable lessons in communication, patience, and acceptance.

This isn't just a book about Amina's story—it's a guide for all of us. It's a reminder that we should approach every relationship, every person, with understanding and empathy. As you read, I encourage you to absorb every word. Take heed of the advice, the lessons, and the guidance offered here. Whether you are neurodivergent or not, learning to understand and accept others—especially in the context of love and relationships—is one of the most powerful gifts you can give yourself and those around you.

Amina's vulnerability in this book will inspire you, and her wisdom will guide you. I am proud beyond words of the woman she is and the message she is sharing with the world. I believe this book will change hearts, change minds, and ultimately, change lives.

## INTRODUCTION

# THE INVISIBLE SPECTRUM: BLACK WOMEN AND GIRLS IN AUTISM RESEARCH

Welcome to a journey that's about to change the way you see the world – and maybe even yourself. Buckle up, because we're diving headfirst into the colorful, complex, and often misunderstood realm of neurodiversity.

But before we get into that, let me tell you a story. It's a story that hits close to home for many, including myself and countless others whose experiences have been hidden in plain sight. For nineteen years, my life, much like the life of Bria Herbert, was shrouded in misunderstanding and missed signals, my true self obscured by layers of societal prejudice. As a young Black woman, Bria's autism went unnoticed, and her behaviors were misinterpreted through the lens of racial and gender stereotypes. Her quiet nature was seen as aloofness, her intense interests labeled as peculiar, and her social struggles dismissed as mere shyness.

In a system designed to recognize autism in White boys, our experiences as Black women were both unique and painfully similar to many others. Bria's journey, like mine, from confusion to clarity, from misunderstanding to diagnosis, shines a light on paths too often hidden in darkness. It's a story that challenges us to look beyond biases and see the diverse ways neurodiversity presents itself across all communities. But it's not just about personal victory – it's a call for societal change.

You see, despite the billions invested in autism research and education, the stories of Black autistic women and girls remain overlooked, hidden in plain sight. A 2017 study revealed that Black children are consistently diagnosed later than their White peers, delaying crucial early intervention and perpetuating misunderstandings. This systemic oversight has led to widespread underdiagnosis or misdiagnosis, depriving many of the support and recognition they need to thrive.

Hidden in Plain Sight: A Journey of Autism, Motherhood, and Self-Discovery is a celebration of the human mind in all its wonderful, wacky, and downright ingenious forms. It's part memoir, part guide, and all heart. This is the story of my own journey as a Black woman discovering my neurodivergence later in life, intertwined with my experiences as a mother to a neurodivergent child. But it's so much more than that – it's a love letter to all the square pegs in a world of round holes, and a rallying cry for understanding, inclusion, and acceptance.

Being neurodivergent isn't a weakness; it's a superpower. And this book is here to pull back the curtain on the hidden spectrum of neurodiversity that surrounds us. We're going to explore how many world-changing ideas, innovations, and works of art have come from neurodivergent minds – minds that think, perceive, and interact with the world differently, and often, brilliantly.

For every famous neurodivergent person we can name – from Einstein to Simone Biles – there are countless others walking among us, their brilliance often unrecognized and unsupported. They're the coworkers who come up with out-of-the-box solutions, the artists whose work makes you see the world in a new light, the friends who notice details others miss. And too often, their potential is overshadowed by a society that doesn't quite get it.

But this book isn't just about famous names; it's about recognizing neurodiversity in our everyday lives, understanding your quirky cousin, supporting your differently-wired child, and discovering hidden aspects of yourself. It's about action, not just awareness. It's for parents, partners, and educators who want to support neurodivergent individuals, and for those who've always felt a little different but never knew why.

By embracing a broader, more inclusive approach to autism research and neurodiversity in general, we can build a world where everyone is seen and valued for who they truly are. Together, we can change the narrative. By shedding light on these hidden stories, advocating for inclusive research and support, and recognizing neurodivergence as a strength rather than a deficiency, we can create a more compassionate, inclusive world.

So, let's embark on this journey together – a journey from misunderstanding to celebration, from prejudice to progress. By the time we're done, you'll have the tools to love, support, and champion the neurodivergent people in your life – and maybe, just maybe, you'll discover some hidden superpowers of your own.

Welcome to Hidden in Plain Sight.

# PART ONE: THE JOURNEY OF AUTISM AND SELF-DISCOVERY

# CHAPTER 1

# THE DIAGNOSIS THAT CHANGED EVERYTHING

So, it was May 2017, and my life took a turn I never saw coming. My son was diagnosed with autism. That day is etched in my memory—not just because of the diagnosis itself, but because it marked the beginning of a journey that would completely reshape my understanding of autism and, honestly, of myself.

Before that day, I was your typical optimistic and proactive mom. I knew a lot about child development and was always ready to tackle any challenge head-on. However, the journey to this moment had been a whirlwind of emotions, questions, and sleepless nights. As a mom, I always prided myself on being proactive on knowing what my children needed before they even realized it themselves. But in the months leading up to this appointment, I felt that confidence slowly erode, replaced by a gnawing uncertainty that something was different about AJ.

AJ was always a unique little guy. He had this insatiable curiosity and some quirks that set him apart. He reacted intensely to sensory stimuli and struggled with changes in routine. Even something as simple as a car ride would set him off. Most kids would eventually fall asleep, but AJ would cry uncontrollably as if he were in pain. At the playground, he'd stay in his stroller, showing no interest in playing with other kids or even his sister. We tried everything to get him involved, but he just wouldn't budge. These behaviors, initially dismissed as quirks, became more pronounced as he grew older.

*16*

The pivotal moment came during a routine visit to his pediatrician. AJ was my second child and from my research during my first pregnancy, I knew that by 24 months, a toddler should be using 50 to 250 words and combining words into simple phrases like "more juice" or "want truck." But AJ, at 18 months, wasn't talking or responding to his name. Initially, we thought he might have hearing issues and since he couldn't hear that may be the reason why he would not respond to his name or articulate basic words. Then there was the age-old adage "boys develop slower than girls" that echoed in my head, justifying his regression.

So when AJ's pediatrician mentioned his delayed speech, I just brushed it off with that thought in mind. But then came the diagnosis, and everything I thought I knew got turned upside down. Panic, sadness, and a relentless need to "fix" what I thought was broken overwhelmed me.

During the check-up, the pediatrician's demeanor changed. He got quiet and focused intensely on engaging AJ verbally, which was unlike his usual chatty self. After examining AJ, he looked at us and said, "He is babbling like a baby and should be saying at least 50 words. He's not engaging with me the way a child his age normally should." He suggested we see a specialist immediately. Ash and I were concerned but didn't voice it. My mind didn't immediately go to anything associated with mental health I thought it was something easily fixable; as I think about it the pediatrician didn't allude to the possibility of it being Autism but I'm sure he knew. He just urged us to get an evaluation.

We got an appointment within a week. The evaluation was thorough, involving behavioral observations and detailed family history. After several sessions, the specialist told us that AJ met the criteria for moderate to severe Autism Spectrum Disorder (ASD). In that moment, it was as if all the air had been sucked out of the room. I heard myself ask questions, saw myself

## CHAPTER 1: THE DIAGNOSIS THAT CHANGED EVERYTHING

nodding along as the doctor explained what this meant, but it all felt surreal, like I was watching someone else go through this experience. AJ, still engrossed in his toy truck, seemed a million miles away from the conversation that was about to change his life –

our lives – forever. As the doctor continued to speak, handing me a stack of papers and pamphlets, my mind raced. Autism. The word echoed in my head, bringing with it a flood of emotions – fear, confusion, sadness, and strangely, a hint of relief. Finally, there was a name for what we had been experiencing, an explanation for the behaviors and challenges we had been grappling with.

But with that relief came a tidal wave of questions. What did this mean for AJ's future? How would this affect our family? And perhaps most pressingly, how had I, his mother, missed the signs for so long?

The days that followed were a blur of emotions and activity. I threw myself into research, devouring every book, article, and study I could find on autism. I reached out to therapists, scheduled appointments, and began the process of adjusting our home environment to better support AJ's needs. It was exhausting and overwhelming, but it also gave me a sense of purpose, a feeling that I was doing something tangible to help my son.

But amidst all this action, there were quiet moments of doubt and fear. Moments when I would watch AJ playing alone, seemingly in his own world, and wonder if he'd ever have the kind of friendships and connections, I always envisioned for him. Moments when the weight of responsibility felt crushing when I questioned whether I was equipped to be the mother he needed me to be.

As the weeks turned into months, our new normal began to take shape. We found a rhythm with AJ's therapy sessions, learned to celebrate his unique way of interacting with the world, and slowly but surely, began to see the beauty in our neurodiverse family. The diagnosis that had initially felt like an ending was, in fact, just the beginning of a new chapter in our lives.

Looking back now, I realize that May morning in 2017 wasn't just the day AJ was diagnosed with autism. It was the day my world shifted, yes, but it was also the day I began a journey of my own. A journey of self-discovery, of questioning my own neurodiversity, and of learning to embrace the beautiful complexity of the human mind in all its forms.

As I came down from my adrenaline rush, I remember heading to work and decided to watch videos on the disorder. There was one in particular that gave me anxiety and brought me to tears. There was a family that had video footage of when their child was born and how he was developing normally then one day literally as if he went to sleep and woke up a toddler that was acting like a deaf newborn and at that moment my heart dropped because I had the same experience, and it hit me that this would be a lifelong journey. This moment also encouraged me even more to read every article, journal, study, and watch every video that I could find to gain a better understanding, learn the language, and become informed. Although AJ was just a toddler at the time I jumped ahead to what to expect during his adolescence, teenage years, and adulthood and it was during this research that what I was reading matched up with my own childhood, teen, and adult experiences. My intense focus, my quiet nature, my social struggles. It was a shocking realization, and it took me a while before I said anything to anyone but there was always this looming question in my mind…. am I on the spectrum, and was I left undiagnosed for all these years?

## CHAPTER 2

# REVISITING THE PAST: EARLY SIGNS AND COPING MECHANISMS

Growing up, I was often described as a quiet kid who excelled academically. What no one noticed was how much I struggled socially. From a young age, I found solace in books and learning. Diving into subjects with an intensity that was both my strength and my shield, my teachers and parents praised my academic achievements. These achievements became a core part of my identity. Yet, beneath this veneer of success lay a world of silent struggles and unspoken difficulties.

I preferred solitary activities, had specific routines, and engaged in repetitive behaviors that were soothing to me. These were all signs of autism that I unknowingly masked under the guise of being a high achiever. My intellectual abilities overshadowed other concerns, leading everyone to focus on my academic prowess while ignoring my social difficulties. My exceptional grades and high test scores diverted attention from the challenges I faced in social settings.

Research indicates that girls on the autism spectrum often go undiagnosed because they may not exhibit the same behavioral issues as boys. While girls might mask their symptoms by mimicking social behaviors and engaging in quieter, less disruptive activities, boys are more likely to display overt behaviors such as repetitive actions, difficulty with social interactions, heightened sensitivity to sensory input, and a tendency to engage in restrictive interests or routines. This difference in presentation can lead to a disparity in diagnosis rates between boys and girls.

Socially, I was adrift. While other children effortlessly navigated the complex web of friendships and playground politics, I felt like an outsider looking in. I preferred reading, playing computer games, or playing with my cars. (Unlike most little girls, I hated Barbie dolls.) These activities weren't just hobbies; they were my refuge. The predictability and control they offered provided a stark contrast to the chaotic and bewildering social world, with its rules that often made no sense to me.

I had specific routines that I clung to intensely. Each morning, I followed the same sequence of actions, from the way I tied my shoes to the route I walked to school. Any deviation from my routine, no matter how minor, would trigger anxiety and frustration. I remember having the same breakfast—cinnamon and sugar cream of wheat—taking the same route and going to Baskin Robbins every day after school for a single scoop of chocolate ice cream on a sugar cone.

There was one time that I remember specifically while living with my grandmother in Florida. We had a daily ritual of eating cinnamon cakes in the afternoon. One day, she decided to mop the floor around the time we usually had the cakes, which required them to be heated in the oven and I had a complete meltdown. This took my grandmother by surprise because I was usually a quiet, well-behaved child. I ultimately got a butt whooping for being disrespectful and impatient but looking back, I realize I wasn't necessarily upset about not getting the cinnamon bun—it was about having it right then in that moment and the disruption of my routine. Needless to say, after that day, I never ate another cinnamon bun until I was an adult.

As I learned and researched more and more about children on the spectrum I realized these rituals were my way of creating order and stability. The rigidity of these routines provided a framework that helped me navigate daily life. While others might see this behavior as inflexible or obsessive, for me, it was a survival strategy. The consistency of my routines allowed me to manage sensory overload and reduce anxiety, giving me a sense of control in an often overwhelming environment of living in a household with a large number of people. Although I was an only child, I did not grow up in a nuclear family that consisted of two parents and their children. Like most African Americans we had an extended family lifestyle where a household typically consisted of grandparents, parents, aunts, uncles, cousins, and an occasional family friend from time to time if someone needed a temporary place to stay.

Living in an extended family structure brought both benefits and challenges. This network fostered a sense of belonging and community, which was incredibly valuable because it allowed me to feel less isolated. However, for a child with ASD, this environment could also be overwhelming. The constant movement, varied routines, and multiple interactions were difficult to navigate. Sensory overload was a frequent challenge, with the hustle and bustle of a busy household often leading to heightened anxiety. I remember I would always retreat to the one area of the house that no one went to unless it was necessary and that was the bathroom. I would go in there and sometimes just sit on the side of the tub, find something to do with my hair, or read a book until someone knocked.

Having so many people around also meant there was less predictability in daily life. Family gatherings, spontaneous visits, and shared living spaces disrupted the routines that were so crucial for maintaining my sense of order and stability. Each family member had different expectations and ways of interacting, which added layers of complexity to social interactions and communication.

Despite these challenges, my extended family played a crucial role in my development. They provided diverse social experiences and taught me how to adapt to different personalities and situations. In hindsight, the love and support from my extended family were instrumental in helping me navigate a neurotypical world, even though it wasn't something we were aware of, I believe if I did not have access to the different personalities and dynamics that presented themselves between both my maternal and paternal family structures I would have had a really difficult time figuring out how to navigate through the world.Top of FormBottom of Form

Self-soothing behaviors also played a significant role in my childhood. I had this habit of biting the skin off my fingers—a habit that was both painful and comforting. At the time I didn't know why I did it and would always even question why I was doing it but regardless of those thoughts, I did not stop. I now know this ritual helped me manage intense emotions and stress that I couldn't articulate. As I grew older, this behavior transitioned to biting the inside of my cheek because I was getting too old to explain why there were visible bite marks around my fingers and the inside of my cheek provided a subtler but equally effective method of self-soothing.

Understanding these behaviors in the context of autism has been liberating. It reframed my actions not as peculiar or harmful but as necessary tools for coping. I never thought back to those behaviors throughout my adulthood, but when I did, I recall knowing something was different. It didn't help that I also struggled with communicating my feelings and didn't have the language to even question it or bring it to anyone's attention. Yet, because I channeled my focus into academic excellence, these signs were easily overlooked. My family and teachers saw a high-achiever, a student who consistently produced exceptional work and scored in the top percentiles. My intellectual abilities acted as a mask, concealing the underlying challenges.

However, going on this journey of discovery and learning more about the disorder has allowed me to have a newfound understanding helping me recognize those actions as my way of managing overwhelming situations, and bringing a sense of acceptance and self-compassion I had never experienced before.

The masking of my autism was further complicated by gender biases in how autism spectrum disorders are recognized and diagnosed. Studies show that girls on the autism spectrum often remain undiagnosed because their behaviors differ from those typically observed in boys. While boys with autism are more likely to exhibit noticeable behaviors such as hyperactivity or disruptions that catch the attention of caregivers and educators, girls often develop sophisticated coping mechanisms. These strategies enable them to camouflage their difficulties, making their struggles less visible and often misunderstood. This disparity in behavioral presentation leads to a significant gender gap in autism diagnosis, where girls' challenges are frequently overlooked or misattributed.

Excelling academically became my way of navigating the world—a strategy to ensure my differences didn't draw undue attention. The societal expectation for girls to be more socially adept and the pressure to conform to normative behaviors meant my social struggles were easily dismissed or attributed to shyness. Teachers and peers praised my achievements without delving deeper into the quiet, isolated world I inhabited.

The emphasis on my academic prowess created a double-edged sword. On one hand, it provided opportunities and recognition that boosted my self-esteem. On the other hand, it diverted attention from my social difficulties, delaying the realization and acceptance of my autism. It was only later in life, through my son's diagnosis and my subsequent self-discovery, that I began to understand the full spectrum of my experiences. My story is not unique; it reflects the experiences of many women who, like me, have navigated life with undiagnosed autism, their true selves obscured by societal expectations and academic success.

**Adapting to Societal Norms**

As I entered my teenage years, the pressure to conform to societal norms became more pronounced. The expectations of dating and social interactions pushed me to adapt my behaviors and suppress my self-soothing habits. This period was marked by a significant amount of masking—a common strategy among autistic individuals to hide their symptoms and blend in with their peers.

Masking involved a deliberate effort to appear "normal" by mimicking the behaviors and social cues of those around me. I learned to smile when expected, make eye contact, and engage in small talk, even though these actions felt unnatural and exhausting.

This adaptation process was a double-edged sword. On one hand, it allowed me to navigate social situations more effectively and avoid standing out. On the other hand, it came at a significant cost. The constant effort to maintain the façade of normalcy was mentally and emotionally draining.

The burden of masking took a heavy toll on my mental health. The constant anxiety of maintaining a socially acceptable appearance meant I could never fully relax. This state of perpetual vigilance led to chronic exhaustion. Despite my outward success in social interactions, I felt increasingly disconnected from those around me.

Research shows that masking can lead to significant mental health issues, including anxiety and depression. The effort to suppress natural behaviors and conform to societal expectations is mentally taxing and can erode self-esteem over time. For me, the price of masking was a profound sense of anger. As I got older, I noticed that I felt angry more often because I recognized that I was not like others. I was trying my hardest to conform and force myself to exhibit neurotypical characteristics, but it never felt natural. It made me mad because, despite having everything else to contribute—I was smart, pretty, and dressed nicely—I could never seem to feel comfortable with the socializing aspects. I fought these feelings of anxiety for many years, trying hard to fix them on my own but could never figure out how to shake them. Eventually, the constant battle became too much to bear, and I could no longer continue masking. But oddly, I had no clue that I was even masking until well into my adulthood. Even without the language and words to describe it, I knew it had to come to an end but with it coming to an end it led to isolation.

Recognizing the impact of masking has been an essential step in my journey toward self-acceptance. Understanding that my social difficulties and need for routine were not flaws but aspects of my autism has allowed me to approach life with more compassion for myself. It has also underscored the importance of creating environments where neurodivergent individuals can feel safe to be themselves without the pressure to conform.

Looking back, I realize my struggles with social interactions were a significant aspect of my autism, even though I did not have a formal diagnosis at the time. The social world, with its unspoken rules and ever-changing dynamics, was a source of constant stress and confusion. For many autistic individuals, especially girls and women, the price of masking is high. The constant need to appear neurotypical takes a toll on mental well-being, leading to a profound sense of isolation and for me frustration.

The effort to conform often leads to forming superficial acquaintances rather than deep, meaningful relationships. The cognitive load of interpreting social cues and engaging in reciprocal interactions in an attempt to mask can be exhausting, making unstructured social settings particularly daunting. This disparity highlights the need for a greater understanding and acceptance of autistic behaviors, allowing individuals to express themselves authentically without the pressure of masks.

As I reflect on my journey, I hope to bring awareness to the nuanced and often overlooked experiences of girls and women on the autism spectrum. By sharing my story, I aim to challenge stereotypes and broaden the understanding of what autism can look like. It is my hope that future generations of girls will be seen and understood for who they truly are, without the need to mask their true selves under the guise of high achievement.

# CHAPTER 3

# MISSED SIGNS AND MISUNDERSTOOD BEHAVIORS

Emotional distress was a profound and often paralyzing experience for me. In moments of intense emotion, particularly distress, I would shut down completely. The world around me would blur into an overwhelming cacophony of stimuli, and my ability to process and respond verbally would dissipate. These instances of muteness were not mere silence but a total inability to articulate my feelings and thoughts. It was as if a switch had been flipped, rendering me incapable of speech.

To those around me, this behavior was seen as "just how I was." My teachers and parents would often describe me as introverted and reserved, attributing my silence to shyness or a contemplative nature. However, this perspective overlooked the deeper, underlying challenges I faced. My muteness in times of distress was not a choice or a personality trait but a profound manifestation of my struggle with communication—a core aspect of autism that went unrecognized.

The Diagnostic and Statistical Manual of Mental Disorders, Fifth Edition (DSM-5), highlights difficulties in communication, both verbal and nonverbal, as key indicators of autism spectrum disorder (ASD). For me, these difficulties were most apparent during emotional crises. While I could manage day-to-day conversations to some extent, my ability to communicate would collapse under the weight of strong emotions. This collapse was not just frustrating but also isolating, as I found myself unable to seek comfort or understanding from those around me.

Teachers, too, were puzzled by my inconsistency—capable of articulating complex ideas in written assignments but often mute during oral presentations or group discussions.

The nonverbal shutdowns were not limited to school. At home, family conflicts could trigger the same response. Arguments or intense discussions would leave me retreating to my room, unable to express my side or seek reconciliation. My family, not understanding the root of my silence, would either give me space or press harder for a reaction, both responses exacerbating my distress.

It wasn't until much later, during my son's diagnosis process, that I began to understand these behaviors in a new light. Learning about autism and its various manifestations provided a framework for understanding my own experiences. The DSM-5 criteria for ASD include deficits in social-emotional reciprocity and nonverbal communicative behaviors used for social interaction.

My shutdowns were classic examples of these deficits, moments where my ability to engage socially and emotionally was severely compromised.

This realization was both enlightening and comforting. It provided a lens through which I could reinterpret my past, not as a series of personal failures or quirks but as part of a broader neurological condition. Understanding that my muteness during distress was a symptom of autism allowed me to approach these moments with more compassion toward myself. It also highlighted the importance of seeking and creating supportive environments that recognize and accommodate these challenges.

Reflecting on these experiences, I recognize the critical need for awareness and education about autism, particularly the less visible aspects such as nonverbal responses to emotional distress. By sharing my story, I hope to contribute to a greater understanding of autism, encouraging empathy and support for those who, like me, may struggle in silence.

Creating spaces where individuals on the autism spectrum feel safe and understood can make a profound difference. Whether in schools, workplaces, or homes, recognizing the signs of nonverbal distress and responding with patience and support can help break the cycle of isolation and frustration. It is through these efforts that we can foster a more inclusive and compassionate society, where every individual is given the opportunity to communicate and thrive in their own way.

As I transitioned into high school and adulthood, these social challenges persisted, but I also began to develop strategies to navigate them more effectively. Awareness of my own needs and limitations allowed me to seek out environments and relationships that were more accommodating and understanding. I found solace in structured social settings, such as clubs and organizations where interactions were guided by shared interests and clear objectives.

In hindsight, understanding these aspects of my social experiences through the lens of autism has been both illuminating and validating. It has provided a framework for understanding the unique challenges I faced and has underscored the importance of creating inclusive environments that recognize and accommodate the diverse needs of individuals on the autism spectrum.

From a young age, social settings were daunting for me. The thought of accompanying my grandmother or mother to social gatherings filled me with a sense of dread. The anticipation of overwhelming environments—crowded rooms, loud conversations, and unfamiliar faces—would trigger an intense anxiety that was difficult to articulate. Each outing felt like stepping into a sensory minefield, where the barrage of stimuli threatened to engulf me.

As a child, these experiences were particularly perplexing. While other children seemed to thrive in social settings, playing and interacting with ease, I found myself retreating into a shell of discomfort. The bustling noise, the myriad of voices blending into an incomprehensible din, the bright lights, and the constant movement were more than just distractions—they were sources of genuine distress. I would cling to my mother's or grandmother's side, my heart racing, desperate to find an escape from the sensory overload.

This overwhelming response to social environments is a hallmark of sensory processing issues often associated with autism. Sensory processing disorder (SPD) can affect individuals on the autism spectrum, making it challenging to filter and manage sensory input. In my case, the inability to process these stimuli effectively led to significant distress, resulting in a strong aversion to social settings.

During these outings, there was often a critical point where the sensory input became unbearable. My anxiety would escalate, and the need to escape would become urgent. I would tug at my mother's sleeve or whisper to my grandmother, expressing my desire to leave.

My family, although supportive, did not fully understand the extent of my discomfort. To them, my reactions seemed exaggerated or inexplicable. They would reassure me that everything was fine, encouraging me to relax and enjoy the event. However, the reassurance did little to mitigate the sensory assault I was experiencing. On many occasions, my distress was dismissed as mere shyness rather than being recognized as a sensory processing issue.

The need to leave social settings early often had social repercussions. It was challenging to form and maintain friendships when I frequently retreated from gatherings. Peers would perceive my early departures as disinterest or aloofness, further isolating me from social circles. Invitations to future events became scarce, as friends and acquaintances grew accustomed to my absence. The cycle of sensory overload and social withdrawal perpetuated a sense of loneliness and exclusion.

Throughout my childhood and adolescence, my frequent need to leave social settings early began to take a toll on my social life. Initially, peers and friends were puzzled by my sudden departure. At birthday parties, school events, and casual gatherings, I would often slip away quietly, unable to handle the sensory overload. My abrupt exits were sometimes noticed, but more often, they went unremarked, leading others to assume I was simply not interested in being there.

This pattern of early departure was not a conscious choice to avoid social interaction. Instead, it was a coping mechanism for the overwhelming stimuli that I couldn't process. The combination of loud noises, bright lights, and constant movement created a sensory environment that was unbearable. As a result, my only viable option was to leave, seeking the quiet and calm that would allow me to decompress.

Unfortunately, my peers did not understand the underlying reasons for my behavior. To them, my early exits were perceived as aloofness or disinterest. They couldn't see the internal struggle I faced or the sensory challenges that dictated my actions. As a result, I was often labeled as antisocial or unfriendly. These misinterpretations further complicated my attempts to form and maintain friendships.

The social repercussions were immediate and tangible. Invitations to events dwindled as my reputation for leaving early became well-known. Friends and acquaintances started to exclude me from their plans, assuming I would either decline or leave prematurely. This exclusion was painful and confusing, as I desperately wanted to be part of the social fabric but was constantly pushed to the margins by circumstances beyond my control.

As I grew older, I tried various strategies to navigate social expectations and mitigate the repercussions of my early departure. I would time my arrivals to coincide with quieter periods of events, hoping to acclimate gradually before the noise and activity levels peaked. I also sought out smaller gatherings, where the sensory input was more manageable, and interactions felt less overwhelming.

Despite these efforts, the underlying issue remained: my sensory processing challenges were not widely understood or accommodated. Social settings continued to pose significant hurdles, and my early exits persisted. The anticipation of sensory overload often overshadowed the enjoyment of social interactions, leading to a perpetual state of anxiety whenever I received an invitation.

## Understanding My Lifelong Struggles Through the Lens of Autism and Sensory Processing Disorders

For most of my life, I had accepted my social difficulties as an intrinsic part of who I was—an introverted, shy, and sometimes awkward person who preferred solitude over social gatherings. I struggled with making friendships, often feeling overwhelmed in crowded or noisy environments. I thought these were just personality quirks, not realizing that they were manifestations of underlying sensory processing issues.

The information I gathered about autism provided a vocabulary and a framework for understanding my experiences. Sensory processing disorders explained why I felt bombarded by stimuli that others seemed to handle with ease. The loud chatter at social events, the chaotic environment of parties—all these sensory inputs that overwhelmed me were not just nuisances but triggers that my brain struggled to process.

This newfound understanding allowed me to reframe my past experiences. Instead of viewing my early departures from social settings as failures, I recognized them as necessary actions to protect my well-being. Each time I left a party early or avoided a noisy gathering, I was not being rude or antisocial; I was managing my sensory overload in the only way I knew how. This shift in perspective was crucial for healing and moving forward.

Reframing my past in light of this understanding brought a sense of compassion for my younger self. I no longer saw my actions as shortcomings but as adaptive responses to an environment that was often too overwhelming. This self-compassion was a crucial step in my journey toward acceptance and healing. It also allowed me to forgive myself for the times I felt I had let others down or failed to meet social expectations.

## The Importance of Raising Awareness

My experience underscored the importance of raising awareness about sensory processing issues and their impact on social interactions. Sensory processing disorders are often misunderstood or overlooked, especially in those who, like me, have learned to mask their difficulties. The more I learned, the more I realized how critical it is for society to recognize and accommodate these challenges.

Raising awareness involves educating not just parents and teachers but also the broader community. Understanding that behaviors such as avoiding eye contact, needing to leave early, or struggling with small talk are not signs of rudeness or disinterest, but rather coping mechanisms for sensory overload, can foster a more inclusive and empathetic society. By sharing my story, I hope to contribute to this broader understanding and encourage others to be more compassionate and supportive.

Armed with this knowledge, I was better equipped to navigate social situations and advocate for myself. I began to implement strategies to manage sensory overload, such as taking regular breaks during social events, seeking quieter environments, and using noise-canceling headphones when needed. These small adjustments made a significant difference in my ability to participate in social activities without becoming overwhelmed.

Additionally, this understanding helped me in my role as a parent. I became more attuned to my son's sensory needs and more effective in advocating for accommodations in his educational and social environments. Recognizing the parallels between our experiences strengthened our bond and provided a foundation for mutual support and understanding.

Understanding autism and sensory processing disorders has been transformative for both my personal growth and my ability to support my son. The realization that my social difficulties were not character flaws but responses to sensory challenges was both liberating and enlightening. It allowed me to reframe my past experiences with compassion and provided a path forward for managing my sensory needs.

By raising awareness and advocating for greater understanding and accommodation of sensory processing issues, we can create a more inclusive society. My journey has taught me the importance of empathy, both toward oneself and others, and the value of knowledge in fostering acceptance and support. Through sharing my story, I hope to contribute to a world where individuals with sensory processing challenges are understood, supported, and celebrated for their unique strengths.

Today, I am committed to advocating for greater awareness and inclusivity for individuals with sensory processing challenges. By sharing my story, I hope to shed light on the often invisible struggles faced by those on the autism spectrum. It is essential for society to understand that behaviors like early departures are not signs of disinterest or aloofness but responses to sensory overload.

Creating more inclusive social environments requires empathy and accommodations. Simple adjustments, such as providing quiet spaces or understanding the need for breaks, can make a significant difference in allowing individuals with sensory sensitivities to participate fully in social activities. By fostering a culture of acceptance and support, we can break the cycle of isolation and exclusion that so many experience.

Through continued advocacy and education, we can work toward a world where sensory differences are recognized and respected. My journey has taught me the value of perseverance and the importance of understanding.

# CHAPTER 4

# MASKING AND NAVIGATING ADULTHOOD

As I transitioned into adulthood, the need to mask my autistic traits became more pronounced. The social dynamics of college and the professional world demanded a level of conformity and social adeptness that was challenging to maintain. Masking, or camouflaging, became a survival strategy to navigate these environments. I adopted several tactics to blend in and minimize the perception of my differences.

Adopting a persona was a significant part of masking. I created a social "mask" that projected confidence and sociability, even though I often felt overwhelmed. This involved rehearsing conversations and anticipating social scenarios to minimize the chances of being caught off guard. This persona helped me navigate social interactions but came at the cost of authenticity and increased anxiety.

In my early career, the professional environment brought its own set of difficulties. Office politics, team meetings, and networking events were minefields that I had to navigate carefully. The unspoken social norms and expectations were challenging to decipher and adhere to. I often felt like an outsider, constantly worried about saying or doing the wrong thing.

The pressure to perform and fit in led to increased masking. I would spend hours preparing for meetings, scripting potential conversations, and practicing my responses. This preparation helped me manage social interactions but left me mentally and physically drained. The constant effort to maintain a façade of normalcy contributed to a growing sense of isolation and burnout.

Social interactions and relationships in adulthood were complex and fraught with difficulties. Maintaining friendships was challenging as my need for solitude and routine often clashed with social expectations. Friends would perceive my need to leave social gatherings early or my reluctance to participate in spontaneous activities as disinterest or aloofness. This led to misunderstandings and strained relationships. I often felt like I had to choose between being true to myself and maintaining friendships, a choice that left me feeling lonely and isolated.

In both friendships and romantic relationships, communication difficulties were a significant barrier. My tendency to take things literally and my directness often came across as offensive. While I did not struggle with understanding social cues, the nuances of indirect communication and idiomatic expressions posed challenges. Research indicates that autistic individuals often experience difficulties with figurative language and tend to interpret statements more literally, which can lead to misunderstandings. This disconnect between intent and interpretation made social interactions mentally taxing, leading to frustration and avoidance of social engagements.

Navigating adulthood with autism requires a delicate balance between masking to fit societal expectations and maintaining one's mental health and well-being. The strategies used to mask autistic traits, while effective in certain contexts, often come at a significant cost. The challenges faced in college and early career highlight the difficulties of adapting to new environments and social dynamics. Social interactions and relationships remain complex and challenging, underscoring the need for greater understanding and acceptance of neurodiversity in all aspects of life.

## CHAPTER 4: MASKING AND NAVIGATING ADULTHOOD

As I continue to navigate adulthood, the journey towards self-acceptance and finding environments where I can be my authentic self is ongoing. Sharing these experiences is a step towards raising awareness and fostering a more inclusive society that recognizes and values the unique contributions of autistic individuals.

# CHAPTER 5

# EMBRACING NEURODIVERSITY - THE MOMENT OF SELF-DISCOVERY AND ACCEPTANCE

The moment of self-discovery was both profound and liberating. It marked the culmination of years spent questioning, reflecting, and seeking answers. The more I delved into understanding autism, the more I saw myself in the descriptions and traits associated with it. It was as if a fog had lifted, revealing a clearer understanding of who I was.

This realization was not immediate. It was a gradual process of connecting the dots from my past and recognizing patterns that had previously gone unnoticed or were misunderstood. The behaviors and traits I had long considered personal quirks now had a name and a context. This moment of self-discovery was not just about finding a label but about understanding myself on a deeper level. It was about seeing the continuity between my past and present and comprehending the core of my identity.

Acceptance came with time. Initially, the revelation was overwhelming. It challenged my self-perception and required a re-evaluation of my life experiences. However, as I processed this new understanding, I began to feel a sense of peace. Accepting my autism meant accepting myself fully, with all my strengths and challenges. It was an acknowledgment that my experiences and ways of interacting with the world were valid and meaningful.

## The Diagnosis Journey: Self-Diagnosis and Clinical Diagnosis

The journey to understanding my autism was multifaceted, involving both self-diagnosis and clinical diagnosis. Initially, my son's diagnosis sparked a journey of self-reflection and exploration. As I researched autism to better understand and support him, I found striking similarities between his experiences and my own. I recognized patterns in my behaviors and challenges that resonated deeply with descriptions of autism.

Self-diagnosis was the first step. It involved extensive reading, engaging with autistic communities online, and reflecting on my life experiences through this new lens. The more I learned, the more it became evident that autism was a plausible explanation for many of my lifelong struggles. Self-diagnosis was empowering, giving me a framework to understand myself better. However, it also came with doubts and uncertainties.

Was I seeing what I wanted to see, or was this a genuine reflection of my reality?

To gain clarity, I sought a clinical diagnosis. The process involved finding a specialist experienced in diagnosing autism in adults, which in itself was a challenge. Many clinicians are more familiar with diagnosing children, and adult diagnosis requires a nuanced understanding of how autism presents differently across the lifespan and between genders. The clinical evaluation was thorough, involving interviews, questionnaires, and sometimes discussions with family members about my early development and behaviors.

The clinical diagnosis confirmed what I had come to believe through self-diagnosis. It provided a formal recognition and validation of my experiences. While the diagnosis didn't change who I was, it offered a sense of legitimacy and a pathway to access support and accommodations. The formal diagnosis was also crucial in helping others understand and accept my autism, providing a concrete basis for discussing my needs and experiences.

## Emotional and Psychological Impact of Self-Diagnosis

The emotional and psychological impact of self-diagnosis was significant. On one hand, there was a sense of relief and validation. For years, I had felt different but couldn't pinpoint why. The diagnosis provided a framework that explained my lifelong struggles and strengths. It validated my experiences and gave me a sense of belonging to a community of individuals who shared similar traits and challenges.

However, this newfound understanding also brought emotional challenges. There was a period of grieving for the years spent feeling misunderstood and isolated. I had to confront the misconceptions and stigma associated with autism, both in society and within myself. This process was emotionally taxing, as it required dismantling long-held beliefs and attitudes about my identity.

Psychologically, self-diagnosis prompted a period of introspection and self-examination. I revisited past experiences with a new lens, understanding them in the context of autism. This re-evaluation was therapeutic but also brought up unresolved emotions and memories. The realization that many of my challenges were not personal failings but part of my neurological makeup was both comforting and disconcerting.

**Embracing My Identity as an Autistic Adult**

Embracing my identity as an autistic adult involved several steps. The first was seeking knowledge and understanding about autism. I immersed myself in literature, attended seminars, and connected with the autistic community. This not only increased my understanding of autism but also helped me see the diverse and vibrant community of autistic individuals.

I also began to implement strategies to manage my sensory sensitivities and social challenges. This included creating a more structured and predictable environment, using sensory tools, and practicing self-care. These strategies helped me manage sensory overload and reduce anxiety, allowing me to navigate the world more comfortably.

Advocacy became a significant part of embracing my identity. I started sharing my experiences and educating others about autism. This advocacy was both personal and public, as I worked to raise awareness and promote understanding in my social circles and the wider community. Advocating for myself and others helped me feel empowered and connected to a larger movement for neurodiversity and inclusion.

**Embracing Neurodiversity**

Embracing neurodiversity has been a transformative aspect of my journey. Neurodiversity recognizes the diverse ways in which the human brain functions, celebrating differences rather than viewing them as deficits. This perspective shift allowed me to see the strengths that come with being on the autism spectrum. My attention to detail, deep focus on interests, and unique problem-solving skills are now seen as assets rather than anomalies.

This chapter of my life is about finding balance and advocating for a more inclusive society. It involves continuous self-acceptance and finding ways to thrive in a world that often feels overwhelming. It also means helping others understand the unique perspectives and contributions that autistic individuals bring to the world. Embracing neurodiversity is about creating a society that values and supports all its members, recognizing that diversity in neurological functioning is a natural and valuable part of the human experience.

This journey of self-discovery and acceptance of my autism has been empowering and enlightening. It has allowed me to reframe my past, understand my present, and look forward to a future where I can embrace my true self. By advocating for neurodiversity and raising awareness, I hope to contribute to a more inclusive and understanding worlds for all autistic individuals.

# PART TWO: A STEP-BY-STEP GUIDE ON HOW TO LOVE AND SUPPORT A NEURODIVERGENT ADULT

# CHAPTER 6

# UNDERSTANDING NEURODIVERSITY: NEURODIVERSITY 101

As we transition from my journey of discovering and understanding autism, we now shift focus to a more practical and supportive approach. Part Two of this book is designed to serve as a guide for anyone who loves and supports a neurodivergent adult. Whether you are a family member, friend, romantic partner, or colleague, this chapter provides tools and insights to help foster meaningful and supportive relationships with neurodivergent individuals.

Our journey toward understanding neurodiversity begins with education and awareness. Through personal experiences and the stories shared in earlier chapters, it's clear that supporting neurodivergent individuals requires recognizing and appreciating their unique perspectives and strengths. This chapter will help you gain the knowledge necessary to support neurodivergent adults in ways that allow them to thrive.

**Neurodiversity 101: Beyond the Labels**

Neurodiversity, at its core, is the concept that neurological differences—such as autism, ADHD, dyslexia, and others—are natural variations in human neurology, not disorders that need to be cured. This perspective shifts the focus away from trying to "fix" neurodivergent individuals and toward understanding and accommodating their unique needs and strengths. The term was coined by Judy Singer, an Australian sociologist, in the late 1990s and has since become a cornerstone of a movement advocating for the acceptance and inclusion of neurodivergent people.

My deeper understanding of this concept transformed how I view both my son AJ and myself. It has helped me realize that many of the challenges we face stem from societal expectations that don't accommodate our different ways of thinking, feeling, and interacting with the world.

**Common Traits and Behaviors of Neurodivergent Individuals**

Neurodivergent individuals often exhibit a variety of traits and behaviors influenced by their unique neurological wiring. While these characteristics can vary widely, there are some common experiences, particularly for those on the autism spectrum:

- **Communication Styles:** Some neurodivergent individuals may communicate differently, such as taking language literally, struggling with non-verbal cues, or preferring written over verbal communication. They may come across as direct or blunt, often preferring clarity over ambiguity.

- **Sensory Processing:** Many neurodivergent individuals have heightened or diminished sensory experiences. They might be hypersensitive or hyposensitive to stimuli such as sound, light, textures, or temperature, which can lead to behaviors that manage sensory overload.

- **Repetitive Behaviors and Intense Interests:** Repetitive behaviors, like rocking or hand-flapping, and deep passions for specific subjects, are common. These behaviors often provide comfort or help manage stress.

- **Social Interactions:** Social interactions can be challenging for neurodivergent individuals. Many may prefer deeper, meaningful conversations rather than small talk and might struggle to interpret social cues.

Understanding these traits helps dispel myths and misconceptions. For example, the pervasive belief that neurodivergent individuals lack empathy is false. While their expression of empathy may differ, they often experience emotions deeply and are capable of profound understanding and compassion.

## The Importance of Accommodations and Inclusivity

One of the most liberating lessons I've learned is that neurodivergent individuals don't need to be "fixed"—society simply needs to be more accommodating. The neurodiversity paradigm moves away from the medical model of disability and instead adopts a social model, which recognizes that many challenges neurodivergent people face come from living in a world that wasn't designed with them in mind.

For instance, AJ's difficulties aren't due to something "wrong" with him. Rather, they arise when he is placed in environments that don't consider his sensory needs or communication style. This realization has been transformative for me. It has allowed me to advocate for changes that support his unique way of interacting with the world, rather than forcing him to conform to norms that don't fit him.

This idea also applies to the workplace. When I began advocating for neurodiversity training at my job, we saw improved communication and more inclusive team dynamics. Everyone benefited, not just the neurodivergent employees.

**Embracing the Full Spectrum of Neurodiversity**

While my personal experience has centered around autism, neurodiversity encompasses a wide range of conditions, including ADHD, dyslexia, and Tourette's syndrome. Each neurotype brings its own set of strengths and challenges. Understanding these differences is crucial not only in supporting neurodivergent individuals but also in recognizing the value that diverse cognitive styles contribute to society.

At a neurodiversity conference, I met Sarah, who has ADHD, and Miguel, who has dyslexia. Sarah described her brain as "a Ferrari engine with bicycle brakes"—able to hyperfocus on tasks she's passionate about but struggling with impulse control and organization. Miguel, meanwhile, spoke about his dyslexia as a unique way of processing information, one that led him to become a successful visual artist.

These interactions reinforced the idea that neurodiversity is about more than autism. It's about recognizing and celebrating all forms of cognitive variation.

**The Strengths and Challenges of Neurotypes**

Every neurotype comes with both strengths and challenges. For example, autistic individuals often possess remarkable attention to detail, pattern recognition, and honesty. However, they may struggle with social communication or sensory sensitivities. ADHD brings creativity and enthusiasm, but managing time and organization can be difficult. Dyslexic individuals might excel at visual thinking but face challenges with written language.

Understanding these strengths and challenges allows us to support neurodivergent individuals more effectively. Providing clear communication and structured environments can help individuals with ADHD thrive. Recognizing that a dyslexic person may benefit from alternative learning methods, like audiobooks or hands-on projects, can open new doors for success.

**Intersectionality and the Broader Context of Neurodiversity**

Neurodiversity intersects with other forms of diversity, such as race, gender, and socioeconomic status. This intersectionality is crucial for understanding the experiences of neurodivergent individuals in marginalized communities. For example, as a Black woman, my own autism was overlooked for years because of racial and gender stereotypes that didn't fit the standard image of what autism "looks like."

Jamal, a Black autistic man I met at a support group, shared his experiences with ableism and racism, illustrating how these forms of discrimination often compound each other. These insights highlight the need for inclusive policies and spaces that consider the unique challenges neurodivergent individuals from all backgrounds face.

**Dispelling Myths and Misconceptions**

As I've navigated my journey with autism and delved deeper into the world of neurodiversity, I've encountered numerous myths and misconceptions about various neurotypes. These misunderstandings can be harmful, leading to stigma, discrimination, and missed opportunities for support and accommodation.

Dispelling these myths has become an important part of my advocacy work, both for AJ and for the broader neurodivergent community.

One of the most persistent myths about autism is the idea that autistic individuals lack empathy. This misconception has been particularly painful for me to encounter, as it contradicts my lived experience and that of many autistic individuals I know. The truth is that many autistic people feel empathy deeply, but may express it differently or struggle to interpret others' emotional states.

I remember a conversation I had with my friend Lisa, a fellow autistic adult, about this myth. She shared a powerful analogy: "It's not that we lack empathy. It's more like we're empathy sponges, absorbing the emotions around us so intensely that it can be overwhelming. We might shut down or struggle to express our empathy in ways that neurotypical people expect, but that doesn't mean we don't feel it."

This resonated strongly with my own experiences. There have been many times when I've felt others' emotions so intensely that I've become overwhelmed and unable to respond in expected ways. Understanding this has helped me explain my reactions to others and advocate for the emotional needs of autistic individuals.

Another common myth is that autism is a children's condition that people "grow out of." This misunderstanding can lead to a lack of support and understanding for autistic adults. In reality, autism is a lifelong neurological difference. While the way it manifests may change over time, and individuals may develop coping strategies, the fundamental aspects of autism remain.

I've encountered this myth in various settings, from well-meaning relatives who ask if AJ will "get better" as he grows up, to healthcare professionals who are surprised to encounter an autistic adult. Educating others about the lifelong nature of autism has been crucial in advocating for continued support and accommodations for autistic individuals of all ages.

A particularly harmful myth about autism is the idea that it's caused by vaccines. This debunked theory has led to dangerous anti-vaccination movements and has distracted from real research into autism and support for autistic individuals. As someone who has extensively researched autism, both for personal and advocacy reasons, I've made it a point to share accurate, scientifically-backed information about autism's causes and nature.

Moving beyond autism, there are numerous myths about other neurotypes that need addressing. For instance, ADHD is often misunderstood as simply being easily distracted or unable to sit still. In reality, ADHD is a complex neurotype that affects executive functioning in various ways.

I recall a conversation with my colleague Alex, who has ADHD, about the misconceptions he faces. "People think I'm just lazy or undisciplined," he shared. "They don't understand that my brain works differently. I can hyperfocus on tasks I'm passionate about, but I struggle with initiating tasks that don't engage me, even if they're important."

This conversation highlighted the importance of understanding the full complexity of different neurotypes, rather than reducing them to simplistic stereotypes.

Another widespread myth is that dyslexia is just about reversing letters or struggling to read. In fact, dyslexia affects how the brain processes language and can impact various aspects of learning and communication. Many dyslexic individuals have strengths in areas like spatial reasoning and creative thinking, which often go unrecognized due to an over-focus on their challenges with written language.

I had the opportunity to learn more about this from Maria, a successful architect with dyslexia, whom I met at a neurodiversity conference. She explained, "My dyslexia isn't just about reading difficulties. It's about how I process information. I struggle with written instructions, but I have an incredible ability to visualize and manipulate 3D spaces in my mind. This ability is what makes me excel in my field."

Maria's story underscored the importance of looking beyond the challenges associated with different neurotypes to recognize and nurture the unique strengths they can bring.

A persistent myth about Tourette's syndrome is that it always involves involuntary swearing (coprolalia). In reality, this symptom only affects a small percentage of individuals with Tourette's. The majority experience other types of tics, both motor and vocal, which can vary greatly in their manifestation and severity.

I learned more about this from Tom, a teenager with Tourette's who spoke at a local neurodiversity event. He shared his frustration with the media portrayal of Tourette's: "Every time I tell someone I have Tourette's, they expect me to start swearing uncontrollably. That's not what it's like for most of us. My tics are mostly physical, like blinking and shoulder shrugging. It's annoying, but it's not the Hollywood version people expect."

Tom's experience highlighted how harmful stereotypes can be, creating misunderstandings that affect how neurodivergent individuals are perceived and treated in society.

Another widespread misconception is that neurodivergent individuals cannot lead independent, successful lives. This myth can lead to lowered expectations and reduced opportunities for neurodivergent people. In reality, with appropriate support and accommodations, neurodivergent individuals can thrive in various aspects of life, including education, career, and relationships.

I've seen this myth challenged time and time again in my own life and the lives of other neurodivergent individuals I've met. From autistic adults in successful careers to individuals with ADHD running their own businesses, the examples of neurodivergent success are numerous and diverse.

One particularly harmful myth is the idea that neurodivergence is something that needs to be "cured" or "overcome." This perspective fails to recognize neurodiversity as a natural and valuable form of human variation. It can lead to harmful interventions that aim to make neurodivergent individuals appear more "normal" rather than supporting their unique needs and nurturing their strengths.

I remember the relief I felt when I first encountered the neurodiversity paradigm, which challenged this "cure" mentality. It was liberating to realize that my brain didn't need fixing – it just worked differently, with its own set of strengths and challenges.

Another myth that needs dispelling is the idea that neurodivergent individuals lack social skills or don't want social connections. While many neurodivergent people, particularly those on the autism spectrum, may struggle with certain aspects of social interaction, this doesn't mean they don't desire or value social connections.

I've experienced this misconception firsthand. People are often surprised to learn that I'm autistic because I've learned to navigate social situations relatively well. However, they don't see the effort and energy it takes for me to do so, or understand that my way of socializing might look different from neurotypical norms.

For AJ, this myth has been particularly challenging. He deeply wants friendships but struggles with the unwritten rules of social interaction. Helping others understand that his social difficulties don't stem from a lack of interest, but from a different way of processing social information, has been crucial in fostering more inclusive social environments for him.

One of the most pervasive myths is that neurodivergence is rare or uncommon. In reality, neurodivergent individuals make up a significant portion of the population. By some estimates, more than 15-20% of people may be neurodivergent in some way. This includes individuals with autism, ADHD, dyslexia, dyspraxia, and other neurological differences.

Understanding the prevalence of neurodivergence is crucial for creating inclusive societies. When we recognize that neurodiversity is a common and natural part of human variation, we're more likely to create systems and environments that accommodate a range of neurological differences.

Another harmful myth is the idea that neurodivergent individuals lack creativity or imagination. This misconception often stems from a limited understanding of how creativity can manifest. Many neurodivergent individuals have unique and innovative ways of thinking that can lead to highly creative outputs.

I've seen this firsthand in AJ's imaginative play and in my own problem-solving approaches at work. Many of history's most creative figures, from Einstein to Van Gogh, are thought to have been neurodivergent. Their unique ways of perceiving and interacting with the world led to groundbreaking contributions in science and art.

A particularly damaging myth is the idea that neurodivergent individuals are savants or have "special powers." While some neurodivergent individuals may have exceptional abilities in certain areas, this stereotype can create unrealistic expectations and overlook the diverse realities of neurodivergent experiences.

I've had to address this myth when people learn about AJ's autism. They often ask if he has any "special abilities" like rapid calculations or extraordinary memory. While AJ does have areas of strength, like many autistic individuals, he's not a savant. It's important to recognize and nurture the individual strengths of neurodivergent people without expecting them to conform to stereotypical "autistic genius" narratives.

Another misconception that needs addressing is the idea that neurodivergence is a modern phenomenon or a result of contemporary lifestyles. In reality, neurodivergence has likely been a part of human diversity throughout our evolutionary history. What's changed is our understanding and recognition of these neurological differences.

I find it fascinating to consider how neurodivergent traits might have contributed to human innovation and survival throughout history. The intense focus of autism, the creative problem-solving of ADHD, the unique perception of dyslexia – all of these could have played crucial roles in the development of human societies.

A harmful myth that particularly affects women and girls is the idea that certain neurotypes, like autism and ADHD, primarily affect males. This misconception has led to underdiagnosis and lack of support for many neurodivergent women and girls.

As a late-diagnosed autistic woman myself, I've experienced the impact of this myth firsthand. Many of my autistic traits were overlooked or misinterpreted throughout my life because they didn't fit the stereotypical male presentation of autism. I've made it a point to share my story and raise awareness about the diverse ways autism can present across genders.

Another myth that needs dispelling is the idea that neurodivergent individuals cannot empathize or understand others' perspectives. This misconception often arises from a limited understanding of how empathy and perspective-taking can manifest differently in neurodivergent individuals.

I've found that many neurodivergent people, myself included, have a deep capacity for empathy and understanding. We might express it differently or struggle with certain aspects of social interaction, but our ability to connect with others and understand their experiences is often profound.

A particularly harmful myth is the idea that neurodivergent individuals are burdens on society. This couldn't be further from the truth. Neurodivergent individuals contribute to society in countless ways, bringing unique perspectives, skills, and innovations to various fields.

From the tech industry, where many companies are recognizing the value of neurodivergent talent, to the arts, where neurodivergent individuals have long made significant contributions, the positive impact of neurodiversity on society is clear.

Another misconception that needs addressing is the idea that neurodivergence is always visible or easily identifiable. Many neurodivergent individuals, particularly those who have learned to mask their traits, may not be obviously different on the surface. This can lead to misunderstandings and lack of support for individuals who don't fit stereotypical ideas of what neurodivergence looks like.

I've experienced this firsthand, with people expressing surprise when they learn about my autism. "But you don't look autistic," is a comment I've heard more times than I can count. It's important to recognize that neurodivergence can manifest in many ways, not all of which are immediately apparent to others.

A damaging myth that affects many neurodivergent individuals is the idea that they are incapable of change or growth. While neurotypes themselves are lifelong, neurodivergent individuals can and do develop new skills, coping strategies, and ways of navigating the world throughout their lives.

I've seen this in AJ's development and in my own journey. We're constantly learning and adapting, finding new ways to leverage our strengths and manage our challenges. It's crucial to recognize this capacity for growth and provide ongoing support and opportunities for neurodivergent individuals throughout their lives.

Another myth that needs dispelling is the idea that neurodivergence is always a negative thing. While neurodivergent individuals certainly face challenges, particularly in a world designed for neurotypical minds, there are also many positive aspects to neurodivergence.

From the ability to hyperfocus and see patterns that others might miss, to unique creative insights and problem-solving approaches, neurodivergence can bring numerous strengths and advantages. Recognizing and nurturing these positive aspects is crucial for supporting neurodivergent individuals and benefiting from the full spectrum of human cognitive diversity.

A particularly harmful myth is the idea that supporting neurodivergent individuals is too costly or difficult for society. In reality, creating inclusive environments that support neurodiversity benefits everyone. Universal design principles that accommodate neurodivergent needs often improve experiences for all individuals. Moreover, the cost of failing to support neurodivergent individuals – in terms of lost potential, mental health issues, and societal exclusion – far outweighs the cost of providing appropriate accommodations and support.

Dispelling these myths and misconceptions is crucial for creating a more inclusive and understanding society. It's about recognizing the full humanity and potential of neurodivergent individuals, challenging stereotypes, and creating environments where all types of minds can thrive.

As I continue my journey of advocacy and education, I'm committed to addressing these myths wherever I encounter them. Whether it's in conversations with AJ's teachers, discussions with colleagues, or public speaking engagements, I strive to provide accurate information and personal insights that challenge misconceptions about neurodiversity.

I believe that by dispelling these myths, we can create a world that not only accepts neurodiversity but celebrates it. A world where AJ and all neurodivergent individuals can be understood, supported, and valued for who they are. A world that recognizes the strength in cognitive diversity and harnesses it for the benefit of all.

This work of myth-busting and education is ongoing. As our understanding of neurodiversity grows and evolves, so too must our efforts to share this knowledge and challenge outdated beliefs. It's a task that requires patience, persistence, and compassion. But with each misconception we address, each mind we open to a more nuanced understanding of neurodiversity, we move closer to a truly inclusive society.

In the end, dispelling myths about neurodiversity is not just about correcting misinformation. It's about changing hearts and minds. It's about fostering empathy and understanding. It's about creating a world where every individual, regardless of their neurotype, has the opportunity to reach their full potential. And that, I believe, is a goal worth pursuing with all our energy and passion.

## Dispelling Myths and Misconceptions

As our understanding of neurodiversity grows, so too must our efforts to dispel harmful myths. Some of the most persistent misconceptions include:

**Myth:** Neurodivergent individuals lack empathy. In truth, many neurodivergent people feel empathy deeply but may express it differently or struggle to read social cues.

**Myth:** Neurodivergence is a disorder to be cured. Neurodiversity advocates for acceptance and accommodation, not "curing" people to fit neurotypical standards.

**Myth:** Neurodivergent individuals cannot lead successful lives**. Many neurodivergent individuals excel in fields ranging from science to art. Their unique cognitive styles often drive innovation and creativity.

**Myth:** All neurodivergent individuals are the same. Neurodivergent individuals are as varied as neurotypicals. Each person's strengths and challenges are unique.

**Creating a More Inclusive Society**

By understanding neurodiversity and embracing the social model of disability, we can create more inclusive environments that celebrate cognitive diversity. Whether in schools, workplaces, or communities, we must move beyond labels to recognize the strengths neurodivergent individuals bring to the table.

In education, this could mean offering different ways for students to engage with material and demonstrate their knowledge. In the workplace, it involves recognizing the value of diverse thinking styles and making accommodations that benefit everyone, not just neurodivergent employees.

## CHAPTER 7

# BUILDING MEANINGFUL RELATIONSHIPS

Effective communication with neurodivergent adults requires a keen understanding of their unique communication styles and preferences. It's important to recognize that these individuals might have different ways of processing and expressing information. Active listening is key—this means giving your full attention, showing empathy, and refraining from interrupting. Patience is equally important, as it allows for the natural pace of the conversation to unfold without pressure.

When communicating, aim for clarity and conciseness. Neurodivergent individuals often appreciate straightforward, unambiguous language. Avoid idioms, metaphors, or abstract expressions that might be confusing. Instead, provide concrete information and ask direct questions. Remember that non-verbal cues such as facial expressions and body language can vary significantly. Being observant and responsive to these cues can help in understanding their comfort level and emotional state.

**Tips for Building Trust and Emotional Intimacy**

Building trust and emotional intimacy with neurodivergent adults requires patience, consistency, and a deep respect for their boundaries. Establishing a safe and supportive environment where they feel understood and accepted is crucial. Here are some strategies to help build meaningful relationships:

**1. Create a Safe Space:** Ensure that the environment is emotionally and physically safe. This means being non-judgmental, validating their feelings, and offering reassurance.

**2. Be Reliable and Consistent:** Consistency in actions and words builds trust over time. Being reliable means following through on promises and being there when needed.

**3. Respect Boundaries:** Understand and respect their need for personal space and time. Everyone has different comfort levels with physical touch and proximity, and it's important to honor these boundaries.

**4. Show Empathy and Understanding:** Demonstrate empathy by trying to understand their perspective. Acknowledge their experiences and emotions, even if they differ from your own.

**5. Communicate Openly:** Foster open and honest communication. Encourage them to express their needs and preferences and be open to discussing any challenges or concerns.

**6. Be Patient and Give Time:** Building trust and intimacy takes time. Be patient and allow the relationship to develop at its own pace.

**Understanding Sensory Needs and Preferences**

Many neurodivergent individuals have specific sensory needs and preferences, which can significantly impact their daily lives. Sensory sensitivities can include heightened reactions to sounds, lights, textures, or smells, while sensory-seeking behaviors might involve a desire for certain tactile experiences or movement.

To accommodate these needs, creating a sensory-friendly environment is essential. This might involve reducing background noise, using soft lighting, or providing access to sensory tools like fidget items or weighted blankets. Understanding and respecting these preferences can enhance their comfort and well-being, making interactions more positive and supportive.

By incorporating these approaches, you can create a foundation of trust and emotional intimacy that supports a strong, meaningful relationship with neurodivergent adults. This not only enhances their well-being but also enriches your own understanding and connection with them.

# CHAPTER 8

# SUPPORTING NEURODIVERGENT ADULTS IN ROMANTIC RELATIONSHIPS

R omantic relationships with neurodivergent partners can be deeply rewarding, but they require a nuanced understanding of each partner's needs and preferences. Communication is the cornerstone of any successful relationship, and this is especially true when one or both partners are neurodivergent. Open, honest conversations about expectations, boundaries, and preferences are essential. These discussions help to clarify each person's needs and ensure that both partners feel respected and understood.

Understanding your neurodivergent partner's unique way of processing information and emotions is crucial. This might mean being more explicit in communication, avoiding idiomatic expressions that can be confusing, and being patient as your partner processes their thoughts and feelings. Neurodivergent individuals may have specific routines or rituals that bring them comfort, and respecting these can help create a stable and supportive relationship environment.

**Strategies for Maintaining a Healthy and Supportive Relationship**

Maintaining a healthy and supportive relationship involves continuous effort, empathy, and understanding. Here are some strategies that can help:

**1. Effective Communication:** Clear and direct communication helps prevent misunderstandings.

Regularly check in with your partner about their feelings and needs. Use "I" statements to express your own needs and concerns without sounding accusatory.

**2. Mutual Respect:** Respect your partner's boundaries and preferences. Understand that neurodivergent individuals might need more personal space or time to recharge.

**3. Education and Awareness:** Educate yourself about neurodiversity and your partner's specific condition. This knowledge can foster empathy and help you respond to their needs more effectively.

**4. Regular Check-Ins:** Schedule regular times to discuss your relationship and any issues that may arise. This can help both partners feel valued and heard, and it provides an opportunity to address any concerns before they become significant problems.

**5. Flexibility and Patience:** Be flexible and patient with your partner. Neurodivergent individuals might have different ways of coping with stress or change, and being understanding of these differences is important.

**6. Seek Support When Needed:** Consider seeking the help of a therapist who specializes in neurodiversity or relationship counseling. Professional guidance can provide valuable strategies and perspectives.

## Addressing Challenges and Celebrating Strengths

Every relationship faces challenges, and neurodiverse relationships are no exception. Here are some common challenges and ways to address them:

**1. Sensory Overload:** Neurodivergent individuals might experience sensory overload, which can lead to stress and withdrawal. Recognize the signs of sensory overload and create a plan to manage it, such as having a quiet space for them to retreat to when needed.

**2. Social Interactions:** Navigating social interactions can be challenging for neurodivergent individuals. Be supportive during social gatherings and respect their comfort levels. It's important to find a balance between encouraging social engagement and respecting their need for solitude.

**3. Emotional Regulation:** Some neurodivergent individuals might have difficulty regulating emotions. Developing strategies together to manage emotional ups and downs can be beneficial. This might include mindfulness practices, physical activities, or specific coping mechanisms tailored to your partner's needs.

**4. Routine Disruptions:** Changes in routine can be particularly stressful. Planning and communicating about changes in advance can help reduce anxiety and make transitions smoother.

Celebrating the strengths and unique qualities that each partner brings to the relationship is vital.

Neurodivergent individuals often have remarkable talents and perspectives that can enrich the relationship. Focusing on these strengths helps to foster a positive and supportive dynamic. For instance, their attention to detail, creativity, or ability to think outside the box can be incredible assets.

By addressing challenges with empathy and a problem-solving mindset, and by celebrating each other's strengths, couples can build a resilient and fulfilling relationship. The key is to appreciate and embrace each other's differences, creating a partnership based on mutual respect, understanding, and love.

**Love Languages for Neurodivergents: Discovering Connection through Unique Expressions of Affection**

In our lives, understanding and expressing love can be as unique as our own personalities. The concept of "love languages," popularized by Dr. Gary Chapman, offers a framework for understanding how we give and receive love. For neurodivergent individuals, love languages can take on even more distinct forms, reflecting personal needs for comfort, connection, and support. Let's explore how love languages resonate for neurodivergent individuals, especially in romantic relationships.

## 1. Infodumping: Sharing Passions as an Expression of Love

For many on the autism spectrum, infodumping—or enthusiastically sharing about a special interest—is a profound act of love. Infodumping is more than simply talking about a passion; it's a way of connecting deeply, of showing vulnerability through something meaningful. For neurodivergent individuals, supporting this love language means engaging with their passion, listening without judgment, and seeing it as an intimate invitation to understand their world.

## 2. Parallel Play: Finding Comfort in Simply Being Together

Parallel play, or "body doubling," is the comfort of being near a loved one while engaging in separate activities. It's a quiet acknowledgment of love—no words or direct engagement required. This approach can be especially meaningful for partners with ADHD, as it offers a comforting presence without the pressure of constant conversation. In neurodivergent relationships, parallel play celebrates the beauty of shared space and silent companionship, where just being together is enough.

## 3. Support Swapping: Building Each Other Up

Support swapping involves partners helping each other with daily tasks or challenges, fostering a partnership based on accountability and shared care. Neurodivergent individuals often benefit from gentle reminders and structured support for things like remembering appointments or completing routines.

This love language emphasizes a mutual exchange of care, where both partners actively support each other's needs, making love a functional and supportive foundation.

**4. Deep Pressure: Seeking Comfort through Physical Reassurance**

For some neurodivergent individuals, physical comfort comes through deep pressure, such as a strong hug or weighted blanket. This sensation can be grounding, providing relief from sensory overload or anxiety. Deep pressure allows neurodivergent individuals to feel secure and supported. In relationships, offering a firm hug or holding a partner close can serve as a powerful reminder that they are loved, cared for, and understood.

## 5. Penguin Pebbling: Giving Small, Meaningful Gifts

Named after penguins' habit of giving pebbles to mates, penguin pebbling in neurodivergent relationships is about giving thoughtful, sometimes unconventional gifts. These gestures can range from sharing a meme that made them laugh to bringing home a small item that reminded them of their partner. This love language isn't about the material gift itself; it's about the thought, the connection, and the message, "I was thinking of you."

These neurodivergent love languages offer a fresh perspective on building connection, empathy, and understanding. They emphasize that love is found in actions big and small, in understanding each other's unique needs, and in celebrating each person's way of expressing care. In neurodivergent relationships, love languages are not only a means of connection but a testament to the creativity and adaptability that define every form of love.

## CHAPTER 9

# FAMILY, FRIENDSHIP, AND SOCIAL SUPPORT

Supporting neurodivergent family members involves creating an inclusive and understanding environment. Families play a crucial role in the well-being and development of neurodivergent individuals. It's important to educate all family members about neurodiversity, which can help reduce misunderstandings and foster a supportive atmosphere. Open communication is key, allowing each member to express their needs and feelings. This helps in building a family dynamic where everyone feels valued and respected.

Research has shown that family support significantly impacts the quality of life for neurodivergent individuals. According to a study published in the *Journal of Autism and Developmental Disorders*, family support can enhance social skills, reduce anxiety, and improve overall mental health. By understanding and accommodating the unique needs of neurodivergent family members, families can create a nurturing environment that promotes growth and happiness.

**Creating an Inclusive and Understanding Family Environment**

An inclusive family environment respects and accommodates the needs of neurodivergent individuals. This includes making sensory accommodations, such as reducing noise levels or providing sensory-friendly spaces. Flexible routines that adapt to the needs of neurodivergent family members can also be beneficial. Understanding each family member's unique ways of interacting and expressing themselves is essential.

For example, some neurodivergent individuals might prefer non-verbal communication methods or require more time to process information. Respecting these preferences and finding effective ways to communicate can strengthen family bonds. Additionally, involving neurodivergent individuals in decision-making processes can empower them and ensure their voices are heard.

**Addressing Sibling Relationships and Family Roles**

Sibling relationships and family roles can be complex in neurodiverse families. Encouraging positive interactions and fostering understanding among siblings is crucial. It's important to educate neurotypical siblings about neurodiversity to help them understand their neurodivergent sibling's behaviors and needs. This understanding can reduce conflicts and promote empathy.

Addressing any conflicts with empathy and providing support to all family members helps in maintaining harmony. Family therapy or support groups can be beneficial in navigating these dynamics. It's also important to ensure that neurotypical siblings do not feel overlooked or burdened by the additional responsibilities that may come with having a neurodivergent sibling.

Creating clear family roles and responsibilities can help in managing expectations and reducing stress. It's essential to recognize and celebrate each family member's strengths and contributions. By fostering a supportive and understanding family environment, families can thrive together, embracing the diversity that neurodiversity brings.

**Being a Supportive Friend to a Neurodivergent Individual**

Being a supportive friend to a neurodivergent individual involves understanding their needs and respecting their boundaries. Friendships are a vital part of social life, offering emotional support, companionship, and a sense of belonging. However, for neurodivergent individuals, forming and maintaining friendships can present unique challenges due to differences in communication styles and social expectations. As a friend, it's crucial to be patient, empathetic, and willing to learn about their unique perspectives and experiences.

Research indicates that neurodivergent individuals often experience social isolation and may struggle with forming close relationships. A study published in the *Journal of Autism and Developmental Disorders* found that individuals with autism spectrum disorder (ASD) frequently report difficulties in making and keeping friends due to misunderstandings and social anxiety. By being a supportive friend, you can help bridge these gaps and provide a sense of stability and understanding.

## Encouraging Social Interaction While Respecting Boundaries

Encouraging social interaction should be done with sensitivity to the neurodivergent individual's comfort levels. It's important to recognize that socializing can be overwhelming for some neurodivergent individuals, and pushing them beyond their limits can lead to stress and discomfort. Instead, focus on creating opportunities for social engagement that align with their interests and preferences. This could include shared hobbies, low-stimulation environments, or small, familiar groups.

Providing a supportive presence during social interactions can enhance their social experiences. For example, being mindful of their need for breaks, accommodating sensory sensitivities, and offering reassurance can make a significant difference. Encouraging them to participate at their own pace and respecting their boundaries helps build trust and confidence.

## Building a Strong and Empathetic Social Network

A strong and empathetic social network provides support and understanding. It is important to foster connections that are based on mutual respect and acceptance, allowing neurodivergent individuals to feel valued and included. Building such a network involves cultivating relationships with individuals who are open-minded and willing to understand neurodiversity.

Encouraging neurodivergent individuals to connect with like-minded peers or join support groups can also be beneficial. These groups offer a safe space where they can share experiences, seek advice, and form meaningful connections with others who understand their challenges.

According to research published in the *Journal of Social and Personal Relationships*, having a supportive social network can significantly improve mental health and well-being for neurodivergent individuals. These relationships provide emotional support, reduce feelings of loneliness, and enhance overall life satisfaction.

# CHAPTER 10

# WORKPLACE INCLUSION AND SUPPORT FOR NEURODIVERGENT INDIVIDUALS

In recent years, the concept of neurodiversity has gained significant traction in the workplace, leading to a paradigm shift in how organizations approach inclusion and support for neurodivergent employees. This chapter explores the multifaceted aspects of creating an inclusive work environment that recognizes, values, and accommodates neurodiversity.

The neurodiversity paradigm posits that neurological differences are a natural part of human variation, not inherently problematic conditions that need to be "fixed." This perspective has profound implications for workplace dynamics and policies. Research by Austin and Pisano (2017) suggests that neurodivergent individuals often possess unique skills and perspectives that can be valuable assets to organizations, particularly in areas such as innovation, problem-solving, and attention to detail.

**Creating an Inclusive Workplace Environment**

An inclusive workplace for neurodivergent employees goes beyond mere accommodation; it involves creating an environment where all employees can thrive. A study by Tomczak et al. (2018) found that flexible work arrangements significantly improved job satisfaction and productivity among neurodivergent employees. Key aspects include:

## Flexible Work Arrangements

- **Offering remote work options**: This can reduce sensory overload and provide a comfortable work environment.
- **Allowing flexible hours**: Accommodating individual energy patterns helps in maintaining productivity.
- **Providing extended deadlines**: Recognizing the need for additional time to process and complete tasks.

## Sensory-Friendly Environments

- **Quiet workspaces or noise-cancelling headphones**: Minimizing auditory distractions can help neurodivergent employees focus better.
- **Adjustable lighting options**: Providing control over lighting conditions can accommodate various sensory needs.

- **Sensory-friendly break areas**: Spaces designed for relaxation can help reduce stress and sensory overload.

## Clear Communication of Expectations

- **Providing written instructions and clear guidelines**: This ensures that all employees understand their tasks.
- **Offering regular check-ins and feedback sessions**: Frequent communication helps address any issues promptly.
- **Using direct and unambiguous language**: Clear communication reduces misunderstandings and increases efficiency.

Recognizing that neurodivergent individuals may have unique working styles is crucial for their success and overall workplace productivity. Providing appropriate accommodations and support significantly improved job performance and retention rates for neurodivergent employees.

**Identifying Individual Strengths**

- **Conducting assessments**: Understanding each employee's strengths and challenges helps in assigning appropriate tasks.
- **Aligning tasks and roles with individual abilities**: This ensures that employees are working in areas where they can excel.

**Providing Necessary Tools and Resources**

- **Assistive technologies**: Tools like text-to-speech software and organization apps can enhance productivity.
- **Quiet workspaces or noise-cancelling equipment**: These accommodations help create a conducive work environment.
- **Visual aids or organizational tools**: These resources support clarity and organization.

Tailoring management approaches to support neurodivergent employees involves several key strategies. First, training managers on neurodiversity is crucial. Educating leaders about individualized support strategies ensures that they can effectively address the unique needs of their neurodivergent team members. Second, encouraging open dialogue about work preferences and needs fosters understanding and builds a supportive work environment. Implementing mentorship programs is another important approach. Mentors can provide valuable guidance and support, enhancing the overall work experience for neurodivergent employees.

## Promoting Neurodiversity Awareness and Training

Promoting neurodiversity awareness and training throughout the organization is essential for creating a truly inclusive workplace. Comprehensive training programs are a foundational element. Mandatory neurodiversity training for all employees promotes inclusivity by raising awareness and understanding. Specialized training for managers and HR professionals equips them with the skills needed to implement effective support strategies. Additionally, integrating neurodiversity awareness into onboarding processes introduces new hires to these important principles, fostering a culture of acceptance from the start. Research by Krzeminska et al. (2019) suggests that organization-wide neurodiversity training can lead to improved attitudes and behaviors towards neurodivergent colleagues.

Fostering a culture of acceptance is another critical component. Celebrating neurodiversity by recognizing neurodivergent individuals as valuable team members helps to create an inclusive environment. Encouraging neurodivergent employees to share their experiences, if they are comfortable doing so, provides platforms for storytelling and enhances understanding. Promoting neurodiversity in company communications and policies integrates these values into the organizational narrative.

**Providing Resources and Support**

Providing resources and support is also vital. Employee resource groups offer a support network for neurodivergent individuals and allies. Counseling or coaching services provide professional support to help employees navigate workplace challenges. Sharing educational materials about different neurotypes increases awareness and acceptance, further supporting an inclusive culture.

**Inclusive Recruitment and Hiring Practices**

Inclusive recruitment and hiring practices are foundational for building a neurodiversity-friendly workplace. Adapting interview processes to include alternative formats, such as written responses and work samples, accommodates different communication styles. Providing interview questions in advance and allowing candidates to bring support persons can make the interview process more comfortable for neurodivergent individuals. Focusing on skills and abilities rather than social conformity during evaluations, and considering non-traditional qualifications and diverse experiences, ensures a fair hiring process. Partnering with specialized organizations, such as neurodiversity employment programs and disability employment experts, enhances recruitment efforts and ensures best practices. A study by Flower et al. (2019) found that adapted hiring processes significantly increased the successful employment of autistic individuals in technology roles.

Organizations must be aware of legal obligations and ethical considerations when supporting neurodivergent employees. Adhering to disability rights legislation, such as the Americans with Disabilities Act, ensures legal compliance. Respecting employees' privacy and confidentiality during accommodation processes is also critical. Ethical practices include avoiding tokenism or stereotyping, recognizing neurodivergent individuals as unique, and ensuring equal opportunities for career advancement. Addressing unconscious biases through staff training helps mitigate potential discrimination.

## Measuring Success and Continuously Improving

Measuring success and continuously improving neurodiversity inclusion efforts is essential for ongoing progress. Establishing metrics to track retention rates, job satisfaction, and engagement of neurodivergent employees helps assess the effectiveness of initiatives. Regular surveys or focus groups provide valuable feedback and insights from neurodivergent employees, encouraging open communication about accommodations and support. Staying informed about new research and best practices in neurodiversity, and participating in industry forums and conferences, ensures that the organization remains at the forefront of workplace inclusion.

Creating an inclusive workplace for neurodivergent individuals is not only a matter of social responsibility but also a strategic advantage in today's diverse and competitive business landscape. By understanding and accommodating different working styles, promoting awareness, and fostering a culture of acceptance, organizations can harness the unique talents and perspectives of neurodivergent employees.

The journey towards true workplace inclusion is ongoing and requires commitment at all levels of an organization. As our understanding of neurodiversity continues to evolve, so too must our workplace practices and policies. By embracing neurodiversity, organizations can create richer, more innovative, and more productive work environments that benefit all employees, regardless of their neurological makeup.

## CHAPTER 11

# ADVOCACY AND ALLYSHIP

Advocacy and allyship for neurodivergent individuals represent a powerful force for social change, extending far beyond personal support to create broader societal impact. Advocacy in the context of neurodiversity involves actively promoting the rights, inclusion, and understanding of neurodivergent individuals. Allyship, on the other hand, refers to the supportive role taken by neurotypical individuals in this cause. Both are crucial in creating a more inclusive society that recognizes and values neurodiversity.

Research by Botha et al. (2021) highlights that effective advocacy and allyship can significantly improve the quality of life and societal acceptance of neurodivergent individuals. This underscores the importance of these roles in driving meaningful change. The foundations of effective advocacy and allyship begin with education and self-reflection. This involves developing a deep understanding of neurodiversity and its various manifestations, recognizing and addressing one's own biases and misconceptions, and staying informed about current issues and advancements in neurodiversity research. Equally important is the practice of listening to and amplifying neurodivergent voices. This means prioritizing the perspectives and experiences of neurodivergent individuals, creating platforms for them to share their stories, and avoiding speaking over or for them.

Challenging stereotypes and misconceptions is another crucial aspect of advocacy and allyship. This involves actively confronting harmful stereotypes about neurodivergent conditions, educating others about the strengths and capabilities of neurodivergent individuals, and promoting a strengths-based view of neurodiversity. Advocacy and allyship can take various forms, including:

- **Personal Advocacy:** Supporting neurodivergent friends, family members, or colleagues, making personal environments more inclusive and accommodating, and engaging in conversations about neurodiversity in social circles.

- **Community Advocacy:** Participating in local neurodiversity events and support groups, volunteering with organizations that support neurodivergent individuals, and organizing awareness campaigns in schools, workplaces, or community centers.

- **Political Advocacy:** Engaging with policymakers on neurodiversity issues, participating in legislative processes related to disability rights and inclusion, and supporting political candidates who prioritize neurodiversity and disability rights.

- **Online Advocacy:** Sharing accurate information about neurodiversity on social media platforms, participating in online forums and discussions, and creating or contributing to blogs, podcasts, or videos about neurodiversity.

Engaging with neurodiversity movements and initiatives is a key aspect of effective advocacy and allyship. This involves identifying key organizations, researching established neurodiversity advocacy groups, and understanding the specific focus and approach of different organizations. Active participation in these movements can take the form of attending events, conferences, and workshops on neurodiversity, contributing time, skills, or resources to neurodiversity initiatives, and networking with other advocates and allies.

Influencing policy changes is one of the most impactful aspects of advocacy. This begins with understanding current policies, researching existing laws and policies related to neurodiversity and disability rights, and identifying gaps and areas for improvement in current legislation. Engaging with policymakers is crucial, which may involve contacting local representatives about neurodiversity issues, providing testimony or evidence to support policy changes, and organizing letter-writing campaigns or petitions. Advocates and allies should focus on promoting inclusive policies, such as advocating for accommodations in educational settings, supporting workplace policies that recognize and value neurodiversity, and pushing for accessible public spaces and services.

It's important to acknowledge the challenges and ethical considerations in advocacy. Advocates and allies must be careful to avoid tokenism and exploitation, ensuring that neurodivergent individuals are not used as props in advocacy efforts and respecting their privacy and autonomy. Navigating diverse perspectives within the neurodivergent community can be challenging, as it requires recognizing the heterogeneity within this group and balancing different viewpoints and needs in advocacy efforts. Maintaining authenticity is crucial, ensuring that advocacy efforts align with the true needs of the neurodivergent community and avoiding performative allyship or surface-level support.

The impact of effective advocacy and allyship can be profound at individual, community, and societal levels. On an individual level, it can lead to improved self-esteem and quality of life for neurodivergent individuals, as well as greater access to opportunities and support. At the community level, it can result in increased awareness and acceptance of neurodiversity and more inclusive community spaces and events. On a societal level, effective advocacy can drive policy changes that promote inclusion and accessibility and shift societal attitudes towards neurodiversity.

Looking to the future of neurodiversity advocacy, several emerging trends are worth noting. There is an increasing focus on intersectionality in neurodiversity advocacy, recognizing that neurodivergent individuals may also belong to other marginalized groups. There's also growing recognition of neurodiversity in various professional fields. Technological advancements are playing a significant role, with advocates leveraging technology for more effective advocacy and support, and developing assistive technologies that empower neurodivergent individuals. The global perspective on neurodiversity advocacy is expanding, with efforts to address neurodiversity on a global scale and foster international collaborations and knowledge sharing.

Advocacy and allyship for neurodiversity represent a powerful force for social change, with the potential to reshape societal norms and create a more inclusive world for all. By understanding the multifaceted nature of these roles, engaging in various forms of advocacy, and working collaboratively towards policy changes, advocates and allies can drive significant progress in the recognition and support of neurodivergent individuals. The journey of advocacy and allyship is ongoing, requiring continuous learning, self-reflection, and action. As our understanding of neurodiversity evolves, so too must our approaches to advocacy. By centering the voices and experiences of neurodivergent individuals, challenging societal norms, and persistently working towards inclusive policies and practices, advocates and allies can contribute to a future where neurodiversity is not just accepted, but celebrated as a vital aspect of human variation. This chapter serves as both a guide and a call to action for those committed to supporting neurodiversity, emphasizing the importance of informed, ethical, and impactful advocacy that respects the autonomy and diversity of the neurodivergent community while striving for meaningful societal change.

## CHAPTER 12

# SELF-CARE AND CONTINUOUS LEARNING

Supporting neurodivergent adults is an enriching journey that requires commitment, empathy, and resilience. Those who undertake this supportive role must also prioritize their own well-being through self-care and continuous learning. This chapter emphasizes the importance of self-care for caregivers and advocates, highlights resources for ongoing education about neurodiversity, and underscores the value of seeking community support.

Self-care is not merely an act of personal indulgence but a necessity for those who support neurodivergent adults. It is crucial for maintaining one's mental, emotional, and physical health. Taking time to rest, recharge, and engage in activities that rejuvenate the spirit ensures that supporters can continue to provide high-quality care while preserving their own well-being. The demands of caregiving can sometimes be overwhelming, making burnout a real risk for those who neglect their own needs.

Self-care strategies might include setting aside time for hobbies, maintaining a regular exercise routine, ensuring adequate sleep, and practicing mindfulness or relaxation techniques. It is also important to recognize when to seek professional help, such as counseling or therapy, to manage stress or emotional challenges effectively. Acknowledging and addressing one's own needs not only prevents burnout but also models healthy behavior for the neurodivergent individuals they support.

Understanding neurodiversity is a dynamic, ongoing process. The landscape of neurodiversity research and practice is continually evolving, with new insights and strategies emerging regularly. Engaging with this ever-changing field requires a commitment to continuous learning.

There are numerous resources available for those interested in deepening their understanding of neurodiversity. Books written by experts in the field, as well as firsthand accounts from neurodivergent individuals, provide diverse perspectives and a deeper understanding of the spectrum. Online courses offer structured learning opportunities that can enhance one's knowledge and skills in supporting neurodivergent adults. Additionally, support groups and community forums can be invaluable, offering up-to-date information, shared experiences, and practical advice.

These resources not only enrich the supporter's knowledge but also equip them with the latest tools and strategies to effectively advocate for and support neurodivergent individuals. They ensure that supporters are well-informed and prepared to adapt to new challenges and changes in the field.

The journey of supporting a neurodivergent adult is not meant to be walked alone. Engaging with a community of others who share similar experiences can provide emotional support, encouragement, and practical advice. Support networks can alleviate the sense of isolation that sometimes accompanies caregiving and advocacy roles.

Finding community can involve joining local or online support groups, participating in workshops and conferences, or connecting with organizations dedicated to neurodiversity. These communities serve as a platform for sharing experiences, exchanging resources, and fostering a sense of belonging among those who might otherwise feel disconnected.

The benefits of community engagement extend beyond individual support; they also contribute to the broader goal of building an inclusive society. By connecting with others, supporters can strengthen their advocacy efforts, share effective practices, and collectively push for changes that improve the lives of neurodivergent individuals.

Caring for neurodivergent adults is a profound responsibility that comes with unique challenges and rewards. By embracing self-care, committing to continuous learning, and seeking support from like-minded communities, supporters can ensure they are well-equipped to provide the best possible care. More importantly, these practices enable them to sustain their efforts over the long term, contributing to a more understanding and inclusive world for neurodivergent individuals. This chapter serves as a reminder and a guide for all who take on the vital role of supporting neurodivergent adults—your well-being is essential, and your efforts are invaluable.

## CONCLUSION

# EMBRACING NEURODIVERSITY

As we reach the conclusion of this journey through the pages of understanding and supporting neurodivergent adults, it becomes clear that the path of neurodiversity is not just about challenges—it is about growth, enrichment, and profound connection. This final chapter reflects on the transformative process of embracing neurodiversity, highlighting the dual journey of self-discovery and motherhood, and outlining the continuous commitment required to truly understand and support neurodivergent individuals.

Supporting a neurodivergent adult, especially as a parent, is multifaceted. It stretches beyond caregiving tasks into personal growth. This journey often begins with uncertainty and fear, but over time, it blossoms into a deep understanding of neurodiversity that enriches both the supporter and the supported. Through daily interactions and challenges, both the neurodivergent individual and their caregivers uncover strengths they never knew they had and forge deeper connections with each other.

This relationship dynamic fosters a unique bond—marked by moments of triumph and understanding—that often extends beyond the familial sphere to touch the lives of others. Personal stories and shared experiences help true acceptance take root, not only within the family but also within the broader community.

Embracing neurodiversity is not a static achievement but a dynamic process of continuous education, adaptation, and growth. It requires a commitment to lifelong learning—not only about the neurodivergent condition itself but also about evolving strategies, therapies, and supports that can enhance the quality of life for those on the spectrum. This learning is not without its challenges, but each obstacle overcome is a step forward in the journey of understanding.

Adapting to new challenges and celebrating successes along the way are crucial aspects of this journey. Each milestone, whether small or significant, is a testament to the resilience and dedication of those who advocate for and support neurodivergent individuals. These achievements should be celebrated not only as personal victories but also as collective advancements in the quest for a more inclusive society.

The dialogue on neurodiversity does not end with the closing of this book. Instead, these pages should serve as a springboard for further action and advocacy. Readers are encouraged to take the insights gained from this text and use them to promote understanding and inclusion in their own communities. By educating themselves and others, advocating for the rights and needs of neurodivergent individuals, and fostering inclusive environments, each person has the power to contribute to a more accepting world.

The role of each supporter, educator, and advocate is vital in shaping a society that not only recognizes but also values the diversity within the neurodivergent community. Through these efforts, we can hope to dismantle the barriers that prevent full participation and appreciation of neurodivergent individuals.

As we look to the future, let us carry forward the lessons of empathy, understanding, and acceptance that have been woven through the narratives of this book. Let us continue to advocate for policies and practices that acknowledge the unique contributions of neurodivergent individuals and strive to integrate them fully into every aspect of society.

## CONCLUSION: EMBRACING NEURODIVERSITY

Embracing neurodiversity is a commitment to celebrating the diversity of the human condition. It is an ongoing dialogue, one that requires patience, dedication, and above all, a deep respect for the rich tapestry of human experience. By committing to this path, we pave the way for a future where every individual is not only seen but truly understood and valued.

This conclusion is not an end but a new beginning—a call to all readers to be champions of neurodiversity in their everyday lives, ensuring that every voice is heard and every life is celebrated in the beautiful spectrum of human diversity. By working together, we can create a world that not only accepts but celebrates the unique and valuable contributions of every neurodivergent individual.

# APPENDIX A

# NEURODIVERSITY GLOSSARY

Ableism: Discrimination or prejudice against individuals with disabilities, including neurodevelopmental differences.

ADHD (Attention Deficit Hyperactivity Disorder): A neurodevelopmental condition characterized by difficulties with attention, hyperactivity, and impulsivity.

Allistic: A term used to describe individuals who are not autistic.

ASD (Autism Spectrum Disorder): A neurodevelopmental condition characterized by differences in social communication, sensory processing, and patterns of behavior or interests.

Asperger's Syndrome: A term previously used to describe a form of autism, now generally included under the broader diagnosis of Autism Spectrum Disorder.

Autism: A neurodevelopmental condition characterized by differences in social communication, sensory processing, and patterns of behavior or interests.

Dyslexia: A learning difference that primarily affects reading and related language-based processing skills.

Dyscalculia: A learning difference that affects a person's ability to understand and work with numbers and mathematical concepts.

Dyspraxia: A neurological condition affecting physical co-ordination and movement.

## APPENDIX A: NEURODIVERSITY GLOSSARY

Executive Functioning: Cognitive processes that enable us to plan, focus attention, remember instructions, and juggle multiple tasks successfully.

Hyperfocus: An intense form of mental concentration or visualization on a subject, topic, or task.

Identity-First Language: A way of referring to neurodivergent individuals that puts the neurotype first (e.g., "autistic person" rather than "person with autism").

Masking: The process by which neurodivergent individuals hide or suppress their natural traits to appear more neurotypical.

Neurodivergent: Differing in mental or neurological function from what is considered typical or normal; not neurotypical.

Neurodiversity: The concept that neurological differences are a normal part of human variation, and should be recognized and respected as any other human variation.

Neurodiversity Paradigm: A perspective that views neurodevelopmental conditions as natural variations of the human genome, rather than as disorders or deficits.

Neurotypical: Having a style of neurocognitive functioning that falls within the dominant societal standards of "normal."

Person-First Language: A way of referring to neurodivergent individuals that puts the person first (e.g., "person with autism" rather than "autistic person").

Sensory Processing: The way the nervous system receives messages from the senses and turns them into responses.

Special Interest: A term often used in the context of autism to describe intense and highly focused interests.

Stimming: Self-stimulatory behavior, often involving repetitive movements or sounds.

Theory of Mind: The ability to attribute mental states — beliefs, intents, desires, emotions, knowledge, etc. — to oneself, and to others, and to understand that others have beliefs, desires, intentions, and perspectives that are different from one's own.

## APPENDIX B

# RESOURCES AND SUPPORT ORGANIZATIONS

Autistic Self Advocacy Network (ASAN): A nonprofit organization run by and for autistic people. www.autisticadvocacy.org

Autism Society of America: A leading source of information and resources for the autism community. www.autism-society.org

CHADD (Children and Adults with Attention-Deficit/Hyperactivity Disorder): A leading resource on ADHD. www.chadd.org

International Dyslexia Association: A non-profit organization dedicated to helping individuals with dyslexia. www.dyslexiaida.org

National Center for Learning Disabilities: Provides information and resources for learning disabilities. www.ncld.org

Wrong Planet: An online community for autistic individuals and their families. www.wrongplanet.net

Autism Women's Network: An organization dedicated to supporting autistic women and non-binary individuals. www.autismwomensnetwork.org

Thinking Person's Guide to Autism: A blog and resource for autism information. www.thinkingautismguide.com

The Dyspraxia Foundation: A charity supporting individuals affected by dyspraxia. www.dyspraxiafoundation.org.uk

ADDitude Magazine: A leading source of information and support for ADHD. www.additudemag.com

Neurodiversity Hub: A resource for neurodivergent individuals in higher education and employment. www.neurodiversityhub.org

# ABOUT THE AUTHOR

Amina Phelps is a devoted wife, mother, and passionate advocate for autism awareness. As a strategic HR leader, speaker, career coach, and fractional HR consultant, she provides services in career development, coaching, interview preparation, résumé writing and review, negotiation, corporate training, change management, and HR consulting. As a serial entrepreneur, she has built several multi-million dollar companies with her husband of 20+ years. Amina is also the founder of the National Association of NeuroDivergent Adults. She shares her deeply personal journey with honesty and compassion, offering hope and encouragement to others. For more information on Amina, you can visit www.AminaPhelps.com, and for more information on the National Association of NeuroDivergent Adults, please visit www.NANDANetwork.org

www.ingramcontent.com/pod-product-compliance
Lightning Source LLC
Chambersburg PA
CBHW070141080526
44586CB00015B/1793